SATHYA JOINED THE ELEMENTARY SCHOOL AT BUKKAPATNAM FOR FURTHER STUDIES.

HE WOULD WALK FOUR KILOMETERS ACROSS THE CHITRAVATI RIVER EVERYDAY TO REACH THE SCHOOL.

SATHYA IS ALWAYS CLEAN AND NEATLY DRESSED.

THE VIBHUTI DOT AND KUMKUM DOT ON THE FOREHEAD GIVES SATHYA A SPECIAL LOOK.

MISCHIEVOUS FRIENDS WOULD THROW 'THORN BALLS' AT SATHYA'S THICK HAIR. SATHYA WOULD RUN AWAY TO AVOID THEM.

POOR SATHYA HAS TO PREPARE BREAKFAST AND LUNCH FOR HIS GRANDFATHER IN THE WEE HOURS AND THEN RUSH TO SCHOOL.

ON THE WAY TO SCHOOL, THE ELDERS IN THE SCHOOL WOULD RAG HIM.

SEE SATHYA IS UNRUFFLED WITH THE RAGGING. HE IS BEARING A BROAD SMILE ON HIS FACE.

HOLD SATHYA! SPLASH RIVER WATER ON HIS CLOTHES.

SATHYA USED TO TEACH SOME OF HIS CLASSMATES IN THE EVENINGS FOR A SMALL FEE. HE CONDUCTED HIS CLASSES IN THE HOUSE OF THE PRIEST AT THE RAMA TEMPLE.

SATHYA TAKES HIS LUNCH IN THE TEMPLE OF GODDESS CHOWDAMMA OUTSIDE THE VILLAGE. IT IS A QUIET PLACE.

I HAVE SEEN HIM HOLDING A GOD'S PICTURE IN HIS HAND AND LOST IN THOUGHT.

THE PRIEST STAYED WITH HIS WIFE AND CHILDREN IN ONE OF THE ROOMS IN LAKSHMINARYANA SWAMI TEMPLE COMPLEX.

HIS WIFE THIPPAMMA WOULD GO ROUND THE TEMPLE AFTER ALL THE FAMILY CHORES ARE COMPLETED, IN FULFILMENT OF HER RELIGIOUS DUTIES.

WHAT IS SATHYA DOING SITTING AT THE BACK OF THE ALTAR.

CURIOUS, SHE STOOD BEHIND THE DOOR WATCHING HIM.

SATHYA SAT BEHIND THE ALTAR. BY WAVING HIS HAND IN THE AIR HE MATERIALISED PUJA MATERIALS.

SURPRISED, THIPPAMMA SLIGHTLY MOVED INSIDE TO GET A CLEAR VIEW OF WHAT SATHYA WOULD DO. HE MATERIALIZED A PHOTO OF SHIRDI SAI BABA. HE ALSO MATERIALIZED FRUITS AND DRY GINGER MIXED WITH POWDER SUGAR AS AN OFFERING FOR THE DEITY.

THEN SATHYA LIT CAMPHOR ON HIS PALM AND OFFERED AARATHI TO THE SHIRDI BABA PHOTO MATERIALIZED BY HIMSELF.

FROM WHERE DID YOU GET THIS SATHYA?

A SHAKTI IN MY HOUSE GAVE ALL.

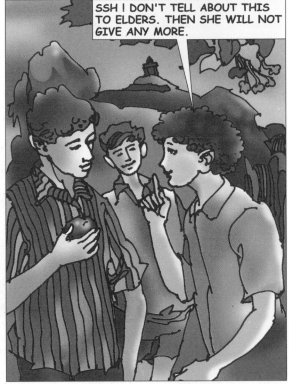

SSH ! DON'T TELL ABOUT THIS TO ELDERS. THEN SHE WILL NOT GIVE ANY MORE.

GARLAND INSTEAD OF FLOWERS

THIPPAMMA'S DAUGHTER, NAGALAKSHMI WOULD PERFORM SHIRDI SAI BABA WORSHIP AT HOME EVERYDAY.

SATHYA WOULD SIT IN THE CORNER OF THE PUJA ROOM TILL THE PUJA IS COMPLETED.

HE WOULD THEN TAKE PRASADAM AND LEAVE.

SATHYA BRINGS FLOWERS EVERYDAY FOR MY PUJA.

FORTY ONE SLAPS

AS A MONITOR SATHYA WAS AUTHORIZED TO PUNISH HIS CLASSMATES, UNDER INSTRUCTIONS FROM HIS TEACHER.

GIVE A SLAP TO EVERY ONE ON THE CHEEK.

ONE DAY THE STUDENTS WERE MAKING LOT OF NOISE DURING A CLASS. THE TEACHER GOT UPSET AND ORDERED SATHYA...

SATHYA NEVER WANTED TO HURT ANYONE. AT THE SAME TIME HE HAD TO OBEY THE ORDER OF THE TEACHER. HE WAS IN A FIX.

FINALLY, HE DECIDED TO FOLLOW THE TEACHER'S ORDER. SATHYA STOOD ON A CHAIR AS HE WAS VERY SHORT.

SATHYA WAS PRETENDING TO SLAP THE FELLOW STUDENTS BUT WAS ACTUALLY JUST TOUCHING THEIR CHEEKS.

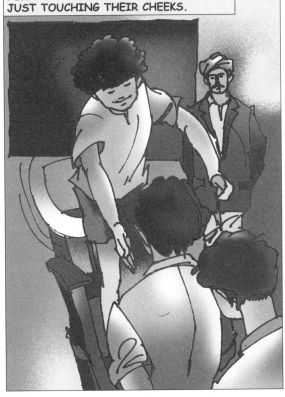

TEACHER GOT WILD AS SATHYA WAS JUST SOFTLY TOUCHING HIS CLASSMATES' CHEEKS.

SATHYA, YOU ARE NOT FOLLOWING MY ORDER PROPERLY. AS A PUNISHMENT YOU TAKE 41 SLAPS FROM ME.

UNFORTUNATELY, SATHYA HAD TO TAKE THE SLAPS.

SATHYA WAS SMILING ALL ALONG.

TEACHER GETS STUCK TO CHAIR

SATHYA IS A VERY GOOD CHILD. HIS STRICT ADHERENCE TO TRUTH AND HIS HUMILITY IS UNMATCHABLE.

I AM SURE SATHYA HAS DIVINE POWERS AND I HAVE SEEN HIM MIRACULOUSLY TAKING OUT THINGS FROM AN EMPTY BAG AND GIVING TO HIS FRIENDS.

OTHER TEACHERS ALSO ACKNOWLEDGED HIS DIVINITY AND THEY TOO HAD OBSERVED SUPER HUMAN POWERS IN HIM.

HE COULD UNDERSTAND EVERYTHING TEACHER WAS TEACHING BEFORE HAND. IT WAS NOT NECESSARY FOR HIM TO GIVE FULL ATTENTION TO THE TEACHER.

DURING CLASSES, SATHYA WOULD WRITE BHAJANS, MAKE COPIES AND DISTRIBUTE TO HIS FRIENDS AFTER THE CLASS.

A NEW TEACHER JOINED THE SCHOOL.

THE NEW TEACHER CAME TO THE CLASS AND STARTED DICTATING NOTES.

SATHYA WAS DEEPLY THINKING ABOUT SOMETHING ELSE. HE WAS NOT PAYING ATTENTION TO THE TEACHER NOR TAKING NOTES.

WHY ARE YOU NOT WRITING ANYTHING?

EXCUSE ME SIR, THERE IS NO NEED FOR ME TO WRITE AND LEARN. PLEASE ASK ME ANY QUESTION-I WILL ANSWER.

WHAT AN IMPOLITE BOY YOU ARE? STAND UP ON THE BENCH.

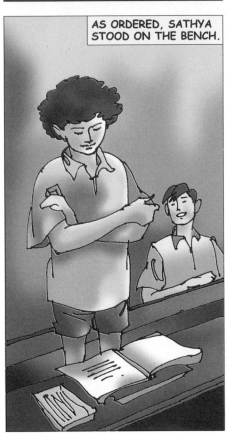

AS ORDERED, SATHYA STOOD ON THE BENCH.

OTHER CHILDREN FELT VERY SORRY, BECAUSE THEIR GURU WAS MADE TO STAND ON THE BENCH.

TEACHER GETS STUCK TO CHAIR

THE BELL RANG. PERIOD GOT OVER. BUT THE TEACHER DID NOT GET UP FROM THE CHAIR.

THE NEXT PERIOD TEACHER MEHBOOB KHAN ENTERED THE CLASSROOM TO TAKE HIS CLASS.

EVEN AFTER THE NEXT CLASS TEACHER CAME, THIS TEACHER DID NOT GET UP.

SIR, IT IS MY CLASS NOW.

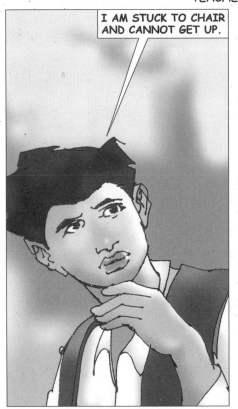

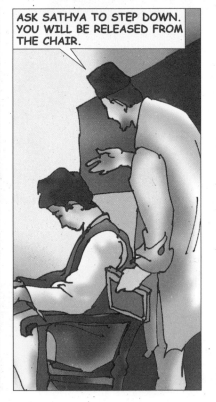

SATHYA, SIT DOWN.

IMMEDIATELY THE TEACHER ALSO GOT RELEASED FROM THE CHAIR.

OH ! SATHYA IS A DIVINE CHILD.

SHIRDI SAI ON THE PALM

SUBBANNACHAR WOULD TEACH ENGLISH TO SATHYA'S CLASS.

ONE DAY SUBBANNACHAR WAS TEACHING GRAMMAR. STUDENTS FOUND THE SUBJECT BORING. THE STUDENTS STARTED PLAYING GAMES.

SATHYA WOULD ALSO NOT PAY ATTENTION TO THE TEACHER AS HE WAS CONTEMPLATING ON SOMETHING ELSE.

THE TEACHER GOT ANGRY AND SHOUTED FOR ORDER IN THE CLASS.

SATHYA, COME HERE!

BEING THE MONITOR YOU FAILED TO CONTROL THE CLASS. BESIDES, YOU WERE ALSO NOT PAYING ATTENTION TO MY LECTURE.

SORRY SIR, IF YOU CAN ASK ME ANY QUESTION, I CAN ANSWER THEM.

NO, YOU WILL BE PUNISHED.

WHEN SATHYA SHOWED HIM THE PALM, SUBBANNACHAR SAW THE FACE OF SHIRDI SAI ON THE PALM OF SATHYA ! THE TEACHER'S HAND WITH THE CANE STOOD IN THE AIR FOR SOME TIME. HE WAS ASTONISHED !

RISHYENDRAMANI

ANNUAL DAY FUNCTION IS APPROACHING. WE MUST DO SOMETHING SPECIAL THIS TIME AS WE WANT TO RAISE FUNDS FOR THE SCHOOL BUILDING.

IT WAS DECIDED TO INVITE FAMOUS DANCER RISHYENDRAMANI FOR DANCE PERFORMANCE AS PEOPLE LOVE TO SEE HER PROGRAMME.

RISHYENDRAMANI IS PERFORMING AT THE SCHOOL. HER DANCE IS ALWAYS WONDERFUL TO WATCH.

YES, PARTICULARLY HER DANCE BALANCING BOTTLE WITH A BURNING WICK ON HER HEAD IS WONDERFUL.

THE WAY SHE PICKS UP THE CRUTCH ON THE FLOOR WITHOUT LOOSING BALANCE AND THE BOTTLE INTACT IS A MARVELOUS FETE.

ALL THE TICKETS ARE SOLD OUT. WE COULD NOT GET TICKET FOR THE DANCE PROGRAMME.

RISHYENDRAMANI IS NOT WELL. SHE IS NOT PERFORMING DANCE TODAY.

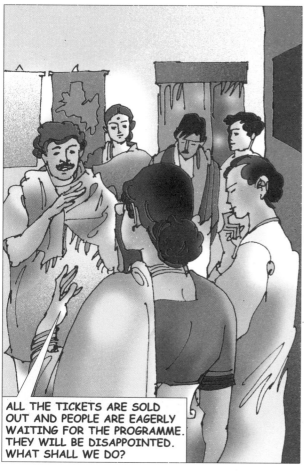

ALL THE TICKETS ARE SOLD OUT AND PEOPLE ARE EAGERLY WAITING FOR THE PROGRAMME. THEY WILL BE DISAPPOINTED. WHAT SHALL WE DO?

MADAM, I WILL PERFORM AS RISHYENDRAMANI.

DON'T WASTE MY TIME. GO AWAY!

PLEASE DO NOT WORRY, MADAM. I WILL DRESS LIKE RISHYENDRAMANI. NO ONE WILL BE ABLE TO SEE MY DISGUISE AND I WILL PERFORM BETTER THAN RISHYENDRAMANI. IF SHE CAN PICK UP CRUTCH FROM THE FLOOR, I WILL PICK UP A NEEDLE WITH THE HELP OF MY EYEBROW WITHOUT LOSING BALANCE.

THERE IS NO CHOICE, MADAM, WE WILL ACCEPT SATHYA'S OFFER.

RISHYENDRAMANI HAS COME. SHE WILL BE PERFORMING A VERY SPECIAL FETE TODAY.

PEOPLE GATHERED IN THE AUDITORIUM AND THERE WAS ENTHUSIASM ALL ROUND.

SATHYA WAS DRESSED LIKE RISHYENDRAMANI. HE WAS LOOKING MARVELOUS JUST LIKE THE DANCER. NO ONE COULD MAKE OUT THE DIFFERENCE.

RISHYENDRAMANI WALKED TO THE STAGE, ACCOMPANIED BY ATTRACTIVE MUSIC, WITH BEAUTIFUL JINGLING SOUND OF HER ANKLETS, SHE STARTED TO DANCE TO THE TUNE OF THE MUSIC.

AFTER A SMALL INTERVAL, RISHYENDRAMANI CAME ON THE STAGE AGAIN. A BOTTLE WITH BURNING WICK WAS KEPT ON HER HEAD.

THE DANCE STARTED. SHE DANCED GRACEFULLY WITH THE ENTIRE SET ON HER HEAD. PEOPLE WERE BAFFLED TO SEE THE PERFORMANCE.

DANCING TO THE TUNE OF THE MUSIC, SHE BENT SLOWLY TO THE FLOOR, WITHOUT DISTURBING THE WICK ON THE HEAD, SHE PICKED UP THE NEEDLE WITH HER EYEBROW AND STOOD UP. THE WHOLE CROWD WENT INTO RAPTURES AND APPLAUDED THE EXTRAORDINARY FETE OF THEIR BELOVED DANCER.

THE BRITISH COLLECTOR, WHO WAS IN THE AUDIENCE, WAS VERY MUCH PLEASED AND WANTED TO PRESENT A MEDAL TO THE DANCER.

INDIAN WOMEN DO NOT ALLOW STRANGERS TO TOUCH THEM. PLEASE GIVE THE MEDAL IN MY HAND !

RELUCTANTLY, THE COLLECTOR GAVE THE MEDAL AND LEFT THE STAGE.

TOMORROW PRIZES WILL BE DISTRIBUTED BY THE PRESIDENT OF DISTRICT BOARD, RAMA SUBBAMMA.

PEOPLE GATHERED AT THE AUDITORIUM TO SEE THE CHILDREN TAKING PRIZES.

I WANT TO PRESENT THIS SAREE TO RISHYEDRAMANI AS HER SCINTILLATING PERFORMANCE HAS BROUGHT GOOD COLLECTION FOR THE SCHOOL FUND!

PEOPLE CLAPPED IN HAPPINESS AND WERE EAGER TO SEE THEIR FAVOURITE DANCER RECEIVING THE GIFT.

TO THE ASTONISHMENT OF EVERYBODY, SATHYA WALKED ON TO THE STAGE.

IT WAS OUR BELOVED SATHYA WHO SAVED OUR FACE YESTERDAY AS RISHYENDRAMANI COULD NOT COME.

THERE WAS THUNDEROUS APPLAUSE IN THE AUDITORIUM.

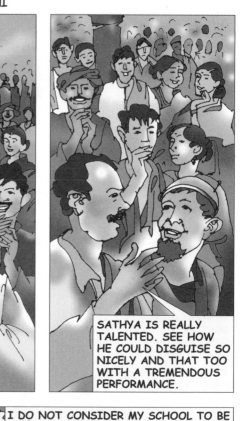

SATHYA IS REALLY TALENTED. SEE HOW HE COULD DISGUISE SO NICELY AND THAT TOO WITH A TREMENDOUS PERFORMANCE.

HE OUTCLASSED EVEN RISHYENDRAMANI.

I DO NOT CONSIDER MY SCHOOL TO BE DIFFERENT FROM MY FAMILY. THAT IS THE REASON I VENTURED TO SAVE THE DIGNITY OF MY SCHOOL.

WILL CARRY WATER OF LIFE

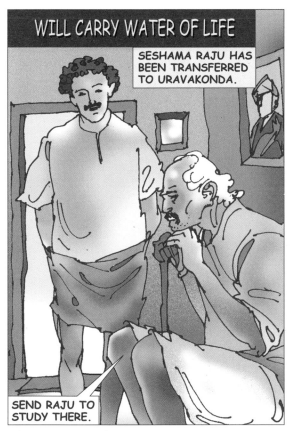

SESHAMA RAJU HAS BEEN TRANSFERRED TO URAVAKONDA.

SEND RAJU TO STUDY THERE.

SATHYA IS A BRIGHT AND SUCCESSFUL STUDENT.

RAJU, YOU HAVE TO BRING WATER FROM THE WELL EVERYDAY.

WITHOUT GRUMBLING, RAJU USED TO BRING WATER IN TWO BIG POTS HANGING FROM A POLE ON HIS SHOULDER. EVEN THE NEIGHBOURS STARTED ASKING RAJU TO HELP THEM. HE USED TO CARRY WATER SIX TIMES A DAY.

CARRYING THE POLE WITH WEIGHT ON THE SHOULDER LEFT A BIG SCAR ON RAJU'S SHOULDER.

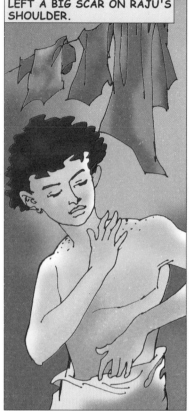

RAJU CAME HOME FOR HOLIDAYS. WHILE ESWARAMMA WAS GIVING BATH, SHE NOTICED LONG AND DEEP SCARS ON SATHYA'S SHOULDERS.

HOW THIS HAPPENED?

DON'T WORRY MOTHER, LEAVE IT.

NO, NO, YOU SHOULD TELL ME HOW IT HAPPENED.

I CARRY WATER ON MY SHOULDERS EVERY DAY FROM A DISTANCE. BUT DO NOT WORRY, MOTHER. IT IS NOT CAUSING ANY PAIN.

I HAVE COME HERE TO CARRY THE WATER OF LIFE TO EVERY ONE. IT IS MY DUTY TO DO THIS SERVICE!

29

DO YOU DO WHAT YOU SAY ?

SATHYA EXHIBITED HIS DRAMATIC SKILLS DURING THE SCHOOL DAYS.

HE ACTED IN BHOOKAILASAM, KRISHNA LEELA, BAYALA NATAKAM AND MANY MORE.

THE MOST FAMOUS OF HIS PLAYS WAS 'CHEPPINATLU CHESTHAARA?' (DO YOU DO WHAT YOU SAY?) WHICH HE WROTE, PRODUCED AND ENACTED.

THE DRAMA EXPOSED THE HYPOCRISY OF TEACHERS AND PARENTS. SATHYA'S DRAMATIC SKILLS ARE ASTOUNDING.

30

DO YOU DO WHAT YOU SAY ?

FATHER IS TELLING SON ABOUT TRUTH. THERE IS A KNOCK ON THE DOOR. FATHER SAYS,

SON, IF THE VISITOR IS SO AND SO, TELL HIM I AM NOT AT HOME !

YOU SHOULD BE ACTIVE IN THE CLASS. NEVER SLEEP IN THE CLASS.

HE WRITES A SUM ON THE BOARD AND ASKS THEM TO COMPLETE THE SUM BEFORE THE BELL RINGS. HE SITS ON THE CHAIR AND FALLS INTO DEEP SLEEP HIMSELF !

THE POOR SHOULD BE FED.

A POOR MAN COMES TO THE DOOR ASKING FOR FOOD AND HE IS ORDERED AWAY BY THE SAME MOTHER !

IT WAS A SCATHING CRITICISM OF THE COMPROMISE ON VALUES MADE BY INSTITUTION OF FAMILY AND SCHOOL.

IT WAS A HILARIOUS SKIT THAT HAD A GREAT IMPACT ON THE ENTIRE VILLAGE.

THE PLAY REFLECTED SATHYA'S DISILLUSIONMENT WITH THE WAYS OF THE WORLD AT THAT YOUNG AGE !